D0876247

Saint Thérèse of Lisieux

And the "little way" of love

Pauline
BOOKS & MEDIA
BOSTON

English edition copyright © 1999, Daughters of St. Paul

ISBN 0-8198-7021-8

Written by Marie Baudouin-Croix

Illustrated by Andrée Bienfait

Translated from the original French by Sr. Maryellen Keefe, OSU

Edited and adapted by Patricia Edward Jablonski, FSP

*Layout:*La 7e HEURE

1998, Éditions du Signe, 1 rue Alfred Kastler, B.P. 94-67038 Strasbourg

Printed in Spain by Beta-Editorial S/A Barcelona

Other titles in this series:

Saint Anthony of Padua
Proclaimer of the Good News

Saint Colette
In the footsteps of Saint Francis and Saint Clare

Saint Francis of Assisi
God's gentle knight

Saint John Bosco
The friend of children and young people

Saint Vincent de Paul
Servant of Charity

This is the story of Thérèse Martin, the little girl who became Saint Thérèse of Lisieux (pronounced *Leez-yur*). Before beginning to read it, turn to the back of the book. There you will find an explanation of some words that may be new to you.

Thérèse wanted to become a saint. And she knew God would help her. She trusted God and loved him with all her heart.

Thérèse never did anything great or special. But she did everything and treated everyone with love. This was the "little way" to God that she discovered.

You can follow Thérèse's "little way" too. Reading her story will teach you how.
It's a sure way to become a saint!

4

You have probably heard of Saint Thérèse of the Child Jesus. She's also known as "Thérèse of Lisieux." But Thérèse Martin was really born in Alençon (pronounced *Al-on-sown*), a lovely town, like Lisieux, in Normandy, France.

Little did the townspeople of Alençon know that Thérèse would grow up to become one of the most popular saints ever....

Thérèse's life on this earth was very short. Born on a cold January 2 in 1873, she was only twenty-four years old when she died in

the Carmelite monastery of Lisieux on September 30, 1897--just over 100 years ago. She never did anything that would make her famous. Thérèse's life was special because it was filled with love.

Thérèse's father, Louis Martin, ran a jewelry and watchmaking shop. Her mother, Zelie, was a skilled maker of "Point d' Alençon" lace. Before long, Mr. Martin sold his store to manage his wife's growing lace business.

Thérèse's birth brought great joy to her parents and to her four older sisters: Marie, Pauline, Leonie and Celine. They were each eager to hold her and help take care of her. The baby made the whole family happy by her smiles.

Since Thérèse was small and sickly when she was born, and Mrs. Martin was not feeling well, Thérèse was sent to live with a family in the country. The farmer's wife nursed her. After a year, the infant returned home with rosy cheeks. She was happy and healthy.

Her father, who called Thérèse "my little queen," set up a swing for her in their yard and everyone enjoyed watching her have fun.

When Mrs. Martin wrote to Thérèse's older sisters who were away at boarding school, she told them about everything Thérèse was doing. Sometimes this included throwing a temper tantrum! But Mrs. Martin patiently corrected her youngest daughter, and little by little Thérèse learned what she should do to please Jesus.

"You should see her praying like an angel," her mother wrote one time. Mrs. Martin was astonished when little Thérèse always begged to go to Mass with the rest of the family.

12

One Sunday afternoon the Martins went to church. Thérèse, tired from a walk, had to stay home. She started to cry, begging for "her Mass," and she finally ran alone toward the church in spite of the pouring rain.

Thérèse loved her family very much. Whenever she climbed the stairs to get to the next floor, she would stop at each step and call out, "Mommy! Mommy!" Then she would wait for her mother to answer her. If Mrs. Martin forgot to answer, Thérèse refused to budge from the step until she did! Thérèse did the same thing with Jesus. She kept calling to him in her heart until he answered.

One day, Leonie, thinking herself to be too old for certain games, put one of her favorite dolls with its clothes, some ribbons and bits of fabric in a basket, and brought it to her younger sisters. "Take whatever you'd like," she said. After Celine had picked out a few ribbons, Thérèse grabbed the basket, crying, "I choose everything!"

Thérèse always remembered this incident. She loved to tell God, "I choose everything that you wish." From the time she was very young, she never wanted to refuse Jesus anything.

Thérèse would later write, "All my life the good God was pleased to surround me with love. My earliest memories are images of smiles and tender kisses.... I also loved Mother and Father who showered me with tenderness in a thousand ways for I was very expressive."

All this happiness suddenly disappeared when Mrs. Martin died of cancer on August 28, 1877. Her five daughters and Mr. Martin were heartbroken. Thérèse, who was only four and a half years old, threw herself into the arms of Pauline, who became her second mother.

From then on her life would be very different.

In November of 1877, the whole family left Alençon. They moved to the town of Lisieux where an uncle and aunt, Mr. and Mrs. Guerin, lived with their two daughters, Jeanne who was nine, and Marie who was seven.

Thérèse played and ran with Celine and her cousins in the huge garden of "Les Buissonets" (pronounced *Lay Bwee-sohn-ay*), a charming house built on a small hill. It was called "Les Buissonets," which means "The Little Bushes," because there were many small shrubs in the yard.

Today great crowds of pilgrims continue to visit this house where Thérèse once lived.

In January 1878, Leonie and Celine started boarding school at Notre Dame du Pre where their two cousins already went. Thérèse stayed home with Pauline, who tutored her.

One day, Mr. Martin brought home a puppy for Thérèse. She named it Tom. Thérèse had hours of fun playing with Tom. Her father would join them whenever he could. He also loved to take Thérèse on walks. Hand-in-hand they would often visit different churches to say "hello" to Jesus.

Sometimes, Mr. Martin took his "little queen" fishing. Sitting quietly on the river bank, Thérèse would think about God. The blue sky, the flowers and trees and all the beautiful things he had created reminded Thérèse of God's great love for her.

After dinner, Mr. Martin and his five daughters would spend the evening in the dining room. What a happy time that was! They sang, told stories, recited poems, and laughed together. Before going to bed, the family prayed before the statue of the Blessed Virgin.

In 1881, Thérèse entered boarding school for the first time with Celine. Some of the other girls were jealous of her, because even though Thérèse was the youngest in her class, she received the best grades. Thérèse suffered very much from this jealousy. She later said, "The five years that I spent in school were the saddest of my life."

The following year, Thérèse became ill because of another sorrow. Pauline, her "little mother," was leaving home to enter the Carmelite convent of Lisieux. It was a big shock to Thérèse. She began to tremble and suffered from terrible headaches. She even "saw" frightening things that weren't really there. Her worried family watched at her bedside.

On Pentecost, 1883, ten-year-old Thérèse had the statue of the Virgin placed near her bed. The Blessed Virgin smiled at her and Thérèse was miraculously cured!

This is how she described what happened: "All of a sudden, the holy Virgin appeared to me. She was more beautiful than anything I have ever seen. Her face radiated goodness and unearthly tenderness, but what moved me in the depths of my being was her ravishing smile. Then all my pain vanished."

Thérèse soon recovered her lively spirit. A year later, on May 8, 1884, she made her First Communion, for which she had been preparing by prayer and little acts of kindness.

Thérèse later remembered: "Oh! How sweet was the first kiss of Jesus to my soul! It was a kiss of love. I felt loved and I told Jesus, 'I love you, and I give myself to you forever.'"

Her First Communion day was doubly happy for Thérèse because it was also the day her sister Pauline made her vows at Carmel and took the new name of Sister Agnes of Jesus. Wearing her white communion veil and dress, Thérèse accompanied her father and her sisters to visit Pauline. Their mother in heaven must have smiled to see her daughters together again on this special day.

After such joyful celebrations, settling back down to schoolwork might have seemed boring. Thérèse, however, was eager to learn and she worked and studied hard.

Then came the happy days of vacation often spent at the seashore at the town of Trouville with Uncle and Aunt Guerin and their daughters. Thérèse loved the immense ocean, the warm sand, and the fun and games!

The Christmas of 1886 was an important one for Thérèse. Coming home from Midnight Mass, she excitedly ran to look for her presents. Mr. Martin was tired. He felt irritated that his thirteen-year-old was acting so childishly. Thérèse overheard him say so. She was ready to burst into tears.

After the death of her mother, Thérèse had become extra sensitive. She cried at the least little thing. The fact that her older sister Marie had also entered the Carmel of Lisieux that October only made things worse.

But in an instant, Jesus changed her heart that night. Thérèse overcame her hurt feelings and happily opened her gifts as if nothing had happened. Later, she would write, "Little Thérèse had regained her strength of soul which she had lost at four-and-a-half, and she would keep it forever.

On this night of light began the third period of my life, the most beautiful of all.... I felt love enter my heart. I needed to forget about pleasing myself, and from then on I was happy."

Thérèse wanted with all her heart to become a Carmelite nun and give her whole life to Jesus. She asked her father permission to enter Carmel in spite of her young age. Mr. Martin said yes, even though it would be a great sacrifice to have Thérèse leave home. Uncle Guerin and the chaplain at Carmel, however, thought she was too young. So did the bishop. He refused permission and advised Thérèse to wait.

But Thérèse wasn't ready to give up. Mr. Martin arranged a trip to Rome for himself and Celine and Thérèse. Afraid of nothing, Thérèse wanted to make this pilgrimage in the hope of obtaining the Pope's permission to enter the Carmelite convent.

At the Vatican, each pilgrim got to meet Pope Leo XIII, but no one was supposed to speak to him. When Thérèse's turn came, she dared to ask her important question. The Holy Father answered, "You will enter Carmel if God wishes it." Thérèse went away in tears.

The pilgrims returned to Normandy with happy memories of the wonders of nature and art they had seen in Italy, Switzerland, and France. Thérèse, instead,

could only think of giving her life to Jesus.
Even when her father suggested making a trip to the Holy Land, she refused. The one place she longed to be was Carmel.

Finally, the bishop's permission for Thérèse's entrance into Carmel arrived! Then the prioress delayed the date. This was a new trial for Thérèse who couldn't wait to give herself completely to Jesus in the great silence of the monastery.

Thérèse used this delay to prepare her heart for a life of love and sacrifice. She held back unkind words. She did little jobs around the house with a smile. She accepted every small opportunity to please God and show him her love.

Thérèse finally entered Carmel on April 9, 1888, taking the name "Thérèse of the Child Jesus." She left behind Les Buissonets, the cozy home she would never see again. She tenderly embraced her family. She said good-bye to Tom.

At the entrance to the monastery, Thérèse knelt before her father to receive his blessing. Full of emotion, the elderly man also knelt down. They tearfully hugged each other. Then quietly Thérèse stood and stepped through the door.

The prioress took her on a short tour of her new home. The excited postulant felt very happy to know that she was in Carmel "forever." The life of prayer and solitude that she had so long desired had finally begun. Thérèse realized her life as a nun wouldn't be easy, but she was ready to accept each difficulty, offering it to Jesus.

At the Carmel of Lisieux, Thérèse found again her older sisters, Marie and Pauline. She never tried to spend more time with them than she did with the other nuns, though. She followed the rule of silence. Even at recreation, she made the sacrifice of speaking more with her other companions than with Marie and Pauline.

The prioress was often very strict with Thérèse because she recognized her courage and wished to make her stronger. The words and actions of certain sisters sometimes hurt her, but Thérèse accepted everything out of love for Jesus. She even made herself help a sister whom nobody else wanted to work with because she was very hard to get along with.

In the community of about twenty nuns, there were different personalities. Not everyone always agreed on the same way of doing things. Thérèse never answered back. She accepted irritations of every kind with a peaceful heart. She only wanted to please Jesus.

On January 10, 1889, Thérèse received the Carmelite habit and the white veil. She added to her name, "Thérèse of the Child Jesus," the new title of "the Holy Face," because she was very attracted to the face of Jesus. She wanted to honor Jesus at both his cradle and his cross. Thérèse also had her cross. Her father had had several strokes, but that day he managed to come to visit her.

Thérèse would later write that nothing was missing on that special day, neither her father, nor even the snow she loved. What a thoughtful gift from Jesus! She said, "I have always wished that on the day of my reception of the habit, nature would be like me--all dressed in white."

A month after this happy celebration, Mr. Martin had to be placed in a hospital for the mentally ill. The picture of the "Holy Face," which represented the face of the sorrowful Jesus, helped to support Thérèse in this suffering. By her letters she consoled her two sisters, Leonie and Celine, who wanted to visit their poor father every day and do whatever they could to help him.

On September 8, 1890, Thérèse made her vows. She wrote a letter to Jesus. Part of it said: "O Jesus, my divine Spouse...let me search for nothing and find nothing but you alone...always be everything for me.... Jesus, allow me to save many souls.... I want nothing but to give you joy and console you."

During a retreat he preached, a Franciscan priest encouraged Thérèse to trust in God's great love and mercy. She later wrote, "This priest launched me in full sail on the waves of confidence and love which had drawn me so strongly, but on which I dared not go."

To make her sisters happy, Thérèse painted religious pictures and wrote poems and plays for community feastdays. She directed the plays and acted in them too!

When Mr. Martin died in 1894, Celine was free to fulfill her dream of entering Carmel. She rejoined her three sisters there. Thérèse helped Celine and taught her to follow the Carmelite Rule. She taught Celine her "little way" of going to Jesus with much confidence and love.

Not too long after, Thérèse became ill. She suffered from a sore throat, a cough, and shortness of breath. Her sister Pauline had become prioress of the monastery. She was now called Mother Agnes. Mother Agnes asked Thérèse to write down her childhood memories. She wanted Thérèse to share the story of God's marvelous work in her life. Thérèse wrote in her notebook, "I will sing the mercies of God...."

On Holy Thursday night, 1896, Thérèse coughed up blood. It was the beginning of a serious lung disease that struck many young people at that time — tuberculosis. Thérèse also found herself surrounded by darkness and doubts. She was tempted not to believe in heaven. She doubled her prayers and her sacrifices. She wanted to show God that no matter what she felt, she loved him and believed in his promise of heaven.

The more Thérèse suffered, the more she trusted in God. She wrote about her desire to please him by being kind to all her companions, even the most annoying. She prayed especially for "poor sinners," so that God's pardon would lead them to believe in his mercy.

These physical and spiritual sufferings lasted for a whole year. Thérèse's only wish was to never stop loving God. She wrote Jesus a beautiful love letter in September, 1896. Here are some parts of that letter:

"To be your spouse, O Jesus, to be a Carmelite, to be by my union with you the mother of souls — that should be enough for me.... But I long for many other vocations. I feel the call to be a warrior, a preacher, an apostle, a doctor of the Church, a martyr.... I would like to do the most heroic things for you, Jesus....

"O Jesus, my Love, I have finally found my vocation. In the heart of my Mother, the Church, I will be love! In this way I will be everything and all my dreams will come true!"

By doing everything out of love, Thérèse was able to help two young missionary priests who were working in far-away lands. One was in Africa, the other in Asia. She prayed for these missionaries, offered little sacrifices for them, and wrote them many letters encouraging them to have confidence in God's never-ending love.

Soon Thérèse became so weak that she had to stop writing. She was sent to the infirmary in July of 1897. In spite of her sufferings, Thérèse was cheerful. She always tried to make her sisters happy and even joked with them. Realizing that she would die soon, she explained, "I am not dying, I am entering into life." She meant that she would find a wonderful new life with God in heaven.

Late in the afternoon of September 30, 1897, Thérèse was in great pain. Her body trembled as she struggled to breathe. She looked up at the statue of the smiling Virgin. Suddenly, grasping her little crucifix, she cried out, "Oh! I love him! My God, I love you!" For several moments her face took on an amazingly bright and beautiful look. Then Thérèse gently closed her eyes. At last she was going to join Jesus, whom she loved so much.

Thérèse had once promised: "I will let fall a shower of roses. I will spend my heaven doing good on earth." Immediately after her death this promise came true. People began receiving the "shower of roses"--many favors and graces that Thérèse asked God to send them.

Thérèse was declared a saint on May 17, 1925. On October 19, 1997, Pope John Paul II proclaimed her a "Doctor of the Church." This means that Thérèse's wonderful example and her teachings about God's merciful love for everyone have spread throughout the world. They have helped many people. Try to keep in your own heart the special words of Thérèse that are the secret of her "little way" to God: "IT IS LOVE ALONE THAT MATTERS!"

A few words to help you better understand St. Thérèse's life...

armel: The religious Order of Our Lady of Mount Carmel ■ **Chaplain:** priest who ministers to a certain group of people ■ **Infirmary:** A place where the sick are cared for ■ **Monastery:** A house where monks or ns live ■ **Pilgrims:** People who travel to a holy place to pray and to el closer to God. The journey they make is called a **pilgrimage** ■ **ostulant:** A person taking his or her first steps in religious life ■ **ioress:** The name given to the superior in a religious Order of women ■ **Recreation:** A period of relaxation in a monastery ■ **Retreat:** A certain time spent in prayer and silence in order to grow closer to God. ■ **ws:** Special promises made to God ■

Prayer

Saint Thérèse,
Help me to come closer to Jesus by following
the "little way" of love.

I want to love Jesus very much.
I want to please him
by treating everyone
as I would like them to treat me.

You always reminded others
of the wonderful truth
of God's never-ending love for us.

Help me to imitate you
and be joyful because I know that God loves me
in a very special way! Amen.

BOOKS & MEDIA

The Daughters of St. Paul operate book and media centers at the following addresses. Visit, call or write the one nearest you today, or find us on the World Wide Web, www.pauline.org

CALIFORNIA
> 3908 Sepulveda Blvd., Culver City, CA 90230; 310-397-8676
> 5945 Balboa Ave., San Diego, CA 92111; 619-565-9181
> 46 Geary Street, San Francisco, CA 94108; 415-781-5180

FLORIDA
> 145 S.W. 107th Ave., Miami, FL 33174; 305-559-6715

HAWAII
> 1143 Bishop Street, Honolulu, HI 96813; 808-521-2731

ILLINOIS
> 172 North Michigan Ave., Chicago, IL 60601; 312-346-4228

LOUISIANA
> 4403 Veterans Memorial Blvd., Metairie, LA 70006; 504-887-7631

MASSACHUSETTS
> 50 St. Paul's Ave., Jamaica Plain, Boston, MA 02130; 617-522-8911
> Rte. 1, 885 Providence Hwy., Dedham, MA 02026; 781-326-5385

MISSOURI
> 9804 Watson Rd., St. Louis, MO 63126; 314-965-3512

NEW JERSEY
> 561 U.S. Route 1, Wick Plaza, Edison, NJ 08817; 732-572-1200

NEW YORK
> 150 East 52nd Street, New York, NY 10022; 212-754-1110
> 78 Fort Place, Staten Island, NY 10301; 718-447-5071

OHIO
> 2105 Ontario Street, Cleveland, OH 44115; 440-621-9427

PENNSYLVANIA
> 9171-A Roosevelt Blvd., Philadelphia, PA 19114; 215-676-9494

SOUTH CAROLINA
> 243 King Street, Charleston, SC 29401; 843-577-0175

TENNESSEE
> 4811 Poplar Ave., Memphis, TN 38117; 901-761-2987

TEXAS
> 114 Main Plaza, San Antonio, TX 78205; 210-224-8101

VIRGINIA
> 1025 King Street, Alexandria, VA 22314; 703-549-3806

CANADA
> 3022 Dufferin Street, Toronto, Ontario, Canada M6B 3T5; 416-781-9131
> 1155 Yonge Street, Toronto, Ontario, Canada M4T 1W2; 416-934-3440